# COOKIES

*Sunset Creative Cooking Library*

By the Editors of Sunset Books

**SUNSET BOOKS**
**President & Publisher:** Susan J. Maruyama
**Director, Finance & Business Affairs:** Gary Loebner
**Director, Manufacturing**
**& Sales Service:** Lorinda Reichert

**SUNSET PUBLISHING CORPORATION**
**Chairman:** Robert L. Miller
**President/Chief Executive Officer:** Robin Wolaner
**Chief Financial Officer:** James E. Mitchell
**Circulation Director:** Robert I. Gursha
**Editor, Sunset Magazine:** William R. Marken

All the recipes in this book were developed and tested in the Sunset test kitchens. For information about any Sunset Book please call 1-800-634-3095.

**The nutritional data** provided for each recipe is for a single serving, based on the number of servings and the amount of each ingredient. If a range is given for the number of servings and/or the amount of an ingredient, the analysis is based on the average of the figures given. The nutritional analysis does not include optional ingredients or those for which no specific amount is stated. If an ingredient is listed with a substitution, the data was calculated using the first choice.

**Nutritional analysis of recipes:** Hill Nutrition Associates, Inc. of Florida.

*Sunset Creative Cooking Library*
was produced by St. Remy Press

**Publisher:** Kenneth Winchester
**President:** Pierre Léveillé
**Managing Editor:** Carolyn Jackson
**Senior Editors:** Elizabeth Cameron, Dianne Thomas
**Managing Art Director:** Diane Denoncourt
**Administrator:** Natalie Watanabe
**Production Manager:** Michelle Turbide
**System Coordinator:** Jean-Luc Roy
**Proofreader:** Garet Markvoort
**Indexer:** Christine Jacobs

*COVER: Black & White Slices (page 53)*

PHOTOGRAPHY
*Darrow M. Watt*

ISBN 0-376-00903-9
Library of Congress Catalog Card Number 94-67311
Printed in the United States

⊕ printed on recycled paper.

# Table of Contents

# Cookie Techniques

Trends in food come and go, but the popularity of homemade cookies never wanes. Easy to make, easy to eat, and appropriate for any occasion, they're favorites with everyone. The key to making successful cookies is an understanding of the basic techniques used in most recipes, shown below. The following tips will help you bake perfect cookies with confidence.

• Before beating the butter and sugar, make sure you start with softened (room temperature) butter.

• Stir dry ingredients together in a bowl; it isn't necessary to sift them unless the recipe directs you to do so.

• When you're ready to bake, always start out with cool baking sheets. Don't grease sheets unless the recipe tells you to do so.

• Always preheat your oven before baking cookies. For best results, bake one sheet of cookies at a time, placing the baking sheet in the center of the oven.

• After baking, transfer cookies to a rack to cool. Arrange them in a single layer, never stacked or overlapped; this lets air circulate around the hot cookies, allowing steam to evaporate and preventing cookies from becoming soggy.

• Let cookies cool completely before moving them.

**Beating batter.** *Beat butter and sugar until light and fluffy to combine thoroughly, and to incorporate air.*

**Chopping ingredients.** *Use a large knife, lifting knife heel in up-and-down movements; steady blade tip with other hand.*

**Preparing to bake.** *For each cookie, drop a scant 1/4 cup dough onto baking sheet.*

# Fillings and Frostings

These fillings and frostings are a flavorful addition to some cookie recipes in this book. For best results, prepare fillings before beginning the cookie recipe; to save time, make frostings while cookies are cooling.

### Date Filling

1½ cups lightly packed pitted dates
½ cup water
2 Tbsp. honey
½ tsp. vanilla
Combine dates, water, and honey. Cook over meduim heat, stirring and mashing, until thick and smooth. Stir in vanilla. Let cool; then cover and refrigerate.

### Fig Filling

1 lb. dried figs (about 2 cups lightly packed)
½ cup walnuts or almonds
⅓ cup sugar
½ cup water
1 tsp. grated lemon zest
2 Tbsp. lemon juice
Using a food processor or a food chopper fitted with a medium blade, grind together figs and walnuts. Turn into a medium-size pan and add sugar, water, lemon zest, and lemon juice. Place over medium heat and cook, stirring, until mixture boils and becomes very thick (5 to 8 minutes). Let cool completely.

### Vanilla Buttercream

¾ cup butter or margarine (softened)
¾ cup powdered sugar
6 Tbsp. marshmallow creme
1 tsp. vanilla
Beat butter, powdered sugar, marshmallow creme, and vanilla until smooth.

### Orange Butter Frosting

4 Tbsp. butter or margarine, softened
2 cups powdered sugar
1 tsp. each vanilla and grated orange zest
2 Tbsp. orange juice
Beat butter and powdered sugar until creamy. Add vanilla and orange zest, beating in enough orange juice for good spreading consistency.

### Royal Icing

1 egg white
⅛ tsp. cream of tartar
Dash of salt
2 cups sifted powdered sugar
Beat egg white, cream of tartar, and salt for 1 minute at high speed. Add powdered sugar and beat slowly until blended. Then beat at high speed until very stiff (3 to 5 minutes).

C O O K I E S

# DROP COOKIES

## Oatmeal Raisin Cookies

*Oatmeal raisin drops are an ever-popular choice for lunchboxes, picnics, and after-school snacks. These are plump, chewy, and delightfully pebbled with oats, raisins, and nuts.*

1 cup (¹/₂ lb.) butter or
   margarine, softened
2 cups firmly packed
   brown sugar
2 eggs
3 Tbsp. lemon juice
2 cups all-purpose flour
1 tsp. **each** salt and
   baking soda
3 cups quick-cooking
   rolled oats
1¹/₂ cups raisins
1 cup chopped walnuts

In large bowl of an electric mixer, beat butter and sugar until creamy; then beat in eggs and lemon juice. In another bowl, stir together flour, salt, and baking soda; gradually add to butter mixture, blending thoroughly. Add oats, raisins, and walnuts and stir until well combined

Drop dough by rounded tablespoonfuls, 2 inches apart, onto ungreased baking sheets. Bake in a 350° oven for 18 minutes or until edges are golden brown. Transfer to racks; let cool. Store airtight.

*Makes about 4 dozen*

# Coconut-Macadamia Cookies

*Although the word cookie comes from the Dutch "koekje,"
meaning little cake, today's cookies often strike a more sophisticated
pose—as in Coconut-Macadamia Cookies, for example.*

1 cup (¹/₂ lb.) butter
   or margarine, softened
¹/₂ cup solid vegetable
   shortening
²/₃ cup granulated sugar
1²/₃ cups firmly packed
   brown sugar
4 eggs
1 Tbsp. vanilla
1 tsp. lemon juice
3¹/₂ cups all-purpose flour
2 tsp. baking soda
1¹/₂ tsp. salt
2¹/₂ cups shredded
   coconut
1¹/₂ cups very coarsely
   chopped macadamia nuts

In large bowl of an electric mixer, beat butter, shortening, granulated sugar, and brown sugar on high
speed until very light and fluffy (about 5 minutes).
Add eggs, one at a time, beating well after each addition. Beat in vanilla and lemon juice. In another
bowl, stir together flour, baking soda, and salt.
Gradually add to butter mixture, blending
thoroughly. Stir in coconut and macadamia nuts.

Use a scant ¹/₄ cup of dough for each cookie.
Drop dough onto lightly greased baking sheets,
spacing cookies about 3 inches apart. Bake in a 325°
oven for 22 to 25 minutes or until golden brown.
Transfer to racks and let cool. Store airtight.

*Makes about 3 dozen*

# Blueberry Lemon Drops

*These summertime treats are at their prime of fragrance and juiciness while still warm, so eat them soon after baking. You can prepare the dough in advance and refrigerate it, then bake the cookies at the last minute.*

⌒

½ cup (¼ lb.) butter
  or margarine, softened
1 cup granulated sugar
1½ tsp. grated lemon zest
1 egg
2 cups all-purpose flour
2 tsp. baking powder
½ tsp. salt
¼ cup milk
1 cup fresh blueberries
Powdered sugar

In large bowl of an electric mixer, beat butter until creamy; gradually add granulated sugar, beating until smoothly blended. Beat in lemon zest and egg. In another bowl, stir together flour, baking powder, and salt; add to butter mixture alternately with milk, blending thoroughly. Gently stir in blueberries.

Drop dough by rounded tablespoonfuls onto greased baking sheets, spacing cookies about 2 inches apart. Bake in a 375° oven for about 15 minutes or until golden brown. Transfer to racks and let cool for 5 minutes; then sift powdered sugar lightly over tops. Serve warm, or let cool completely and store airtight for up to 3 days.

*Makes about 3 dozen*

# Chocolate Cream Cushions

*These tempting soft chocolate
sandwich cookies are filled with velvety
Vanilla Buttercream.*

6 Tbsp. butter or
  margarine, softened
1 cup sugar
1 egg
1 tsp. vanilla
2 cups all-purpose flour
1 1/4 tsp. baking soda
1/4 tsp. salt
5 Tbsp. unsweetened cocoa
1 cup milk
Vanilla Buttercream
  (recipe on page 5)

In large bowl of an electric mixer, beat butter and
sugar until creamy; beat in egg and vanilla. In
another bowl, stir together flour, baking soda, salt,
and cocoa; add to butter mixture alternately with
milk, beating just until smooth.

Drop dough by rounded teaspoonfuls onto
greased baking sheets, spacing the cookies about
2 inches apart. Bake in a 400° oven for 10 minutes
or until firm when lightly touched. Transfer to
racks and let cool completely.

Spread bottoms of half the cooled cookies with
Vanilla Buttercream; top with remaining cookies,
top side up. Store airtight.

*Makes about 2 1/2 dozen*

# Mint Meringues

*These light, dainty cookies are flavored with mint
and studded with chocolate chips. If you like, you can give them a festive
holiday look by tinting them with green or red food color.*

2 egg whites
1/2 cup sugar
1/2 tsp. peppermint or
 spearmint extract
6 to 8 drops green or red
 food color (optional)
1 package (6 oz.) semisweet
 chocolate chips

In large bowl of an electric mixer, beat egg whites
until foamy. With mixer on high speed, gradually
add sugar, about a tablespoon at a time, beating
well after each addition, until whites hold stiff, glossy
peaks. Add peppermint extract and food color
(if used); beat for 1 more minute. Fold in the chocolate chips.

Drop meringue mixture by rounded teaspoonfuls
onto well-greased baking sheets, spacing cookies
about 1 inch apart. Bake in a 200° oven for 1 hour or
until outside is dry and set; cookies should not turn
brown. Let cool on baking sheets for about 5 minutes, then transfer to racks and let cool completely.
Store airtight.

*Makes about 3 1/2 dozen*

# Brownie Date Drops

*Chewy and chocolaty as a brownie,
these soft drops are studded with dates and walnuts
for extra-special flavor and texture.*

½ cup (¼ lb.) butter or
   margarine, softened
1 cup sugar
2 eggs
1 tsp. vanilla
2 oz. unsweetened chocolate,
   melted and cooled
1 cup all-purpose flour
1 tsp. baking powder
½ tsp. salt
1 cup **each** snipped pitted
   dates and chopped walnuts

In large bowl of an electric mixer, beat butter and
sugar until creamy; beat in eggs and vanilla, then
chocolate. In another bowl, stir together flour, baking
powder, and salt; gradually add to butter mixture,
blending thoroughly. Stir in dates and walnuts.

Drop dough by level tablespoonfuls onto greased
baking sheets, spacing cookies about 1 inch apart.
Bake in a 350° oven for 13 minutes or until tops are
dry and just set when lightly touched (cookies will
be soft; do not overbake). Transfer to racks and let
cool. Store airtight.

*Makes about 3 dozen*

# Coconut Macaroons

*If you'd like to enjoy the flavor of both almond and coconut in the same macaroon, try substituting almond extract for the vanilla; you can enjoy the best of both worlds.*

4 egg whites
$^1/_4$ tsp. salt
$^2/_3$ cup sugar
1 tsp. vanilla
$^1/_4$ cup all-purpose flour
3 cups lightly packed
   flaked coconut

In large bowl of an electric mixer, beat egg whites until foamy; beat in salt, sugar, vanilla, and flour. Add coconut and stir until well combined

   Drop batter by rounded teaspoonful onto well-greased baking sheets, spacing cookies about 1 inch apart. Bake in a 325° oven for 20 to 25 minutes or until lightly browned. Let cool briefly on baking sheets, then transfer to racks and let cool completely. Store airtight.

*Makes about 3 dozen*

*C O O K I E S*

# BAR COOKIES

## *Fudge Brownies*

*Whether you're serving family members or special guests, brownies are always winners. This fudgy version will keep everyone coming back for more.*

½ cup (¼ lb.) butter
  or margarine
4 oz. unsweetened chocolate
2 cups sugar
1½ tsp. vanilla
4 eggs
1 cup all-purpose flour
½ to 1 cup coarsely
  chopped walnuts

In a 2- to 3-quart pan, melt butter and chocolate over medium-low heat, stirring until well blended. Remove from heat and stir in sugar and vanilla. Add eggs, one at a time, beating well after each addition. Stir in flour; then mix in walnuts.

Spread batter evenly in a greased 9-inch square baking pan. Bake in a 325° oven for about 35 minutes or until brownie feels dry on top. Let cool in pan on a rack, then cut into 2¼-inch squares. Store airtight.

*Makes 16*

# Bee Sting Bars

*These fancifully named honey-almond bars
come all the way from Germany. They're a favorite of the
Germans, who call them "Bienenstich".*

∞

1 cup (1/2 lb.) firm butter
  or margarine
3/4 cup sugar
2 Tbsp. **each** honey and
  milk
1 cup chopped or slivered
  almonds
1 tsp. almond extract
13/4 cups all-purpose flour
2 tsp. baking powder
1/4 tsp. salt
1 egg

In a small pan, combine 1/2 cup of the butter,
1/4 cup of the sugar, honey, milk, almonds, and
almond extract. Bring to a rolling boil over medium-
high heat, stirring; set aside.

In a mixing bowl, stir together flour, remaining
1/2 cup sugar, baking powder, and salt. Cut remaining
1/2 cup butter into pieces and, with a pastry blender
or 2 knives, cut into flour mixture until mixture is
crumbly and no large particles remain. Add egg and
mix with a fork until dough holds together.

Press dough evenly over bottom of an ungreased
10- by 15-inch rimmed baking pan. Pour almond
mixture over dough, spreading evenly. Bake in a 350°
oven for 20 to 25 minutes or until topping is deep
golden. Let cool in pan on a rack. Cut into 2-inch
squares; for smaller cookies, cut each square diagonally into 2 triangles. Store airtight.

*Makes about 3 dozen squares
or about 6 dozen triangles*

# Buttery Lemon Bars

*These luscious bars will remind you of lemon
meringue pie—minus the meringue topping, and with
a cookie crust instead of pie pastry.*

∽

*1 cup (1/2 lb.) butter or
  margarine, softened
1/2 cup powdered sugar
2 1/3 cups all-purpose flour
4 eggs
2 cups granulated sugar
1 tsp. grated lemon zest
6 Tbsp. lemon juice
1 tsp. baking powder
Powdered sugar*

In large bowl of an electric mixer, beat butter and the
1/2 cup powdered sugar until creamy; beat in 2 cups
of the flour, blending thoroughly. Spread mixture
evenly over bottom of a well-greased 9- by 13-inch
baking pan. Bake in a 350° oven for 20 minutes.

Meanwhile, in small bowl of mixer, beat eggs until
light. Gradually add granulated sugar, beating until
mixture is thick and lemon-colored. Add lemon zest,
lemon juice, remaining 1/3 cup flour, and baking
powder; beat until smooth.

Pour lemon mixture over hot baked crust and
return to oven; bake for 15 to 20 minutes or until
topping is pale golden. While still warm, sift powdered sugar lightly over top, let cool. To serve, cut
into bars about 2 1/4 by 2 1/2 inches. Store airtight.

*Makes about 20*

# Chocolate Oatmeal Peanut Bars

These chewy, candylike bar cookies feature
a creamy topping of chocolate and peanut butter over an oatmeal crust;
a sprinkling of chopped peanuts makes a decorative crowning touch.

2/3 cup butter or
  margarine, softened
1/2 cup firmly packed
  brown sugar
1/2 cup light corn syrup
2 tsp. vanilla
4 cups quick-cooking
  rolled oats
1 package (6 oz.) semisweet
  chocolate chips
2/3 cup creamy peanut butter
1/3 cup chopped dry-roasted
  peanuts

In large bowl of an electric mixer, beat butter and sugar until creamy; stir in corn syrup, vanilla, and oats, blending thoroughly. Pat dough evenly over bottom of a greased 9- by 13-inch baking pan. Bake in a 350° oven for about 20 minutes or until golden around edges; let cool in pan on a rack, then cover and refrigerate until cold.

Meanwhile, place chocolate chips and peanut butter in a 1 1/2- to 2-quart pan. Stir over very low heat until melted and smooth. Spread mixture evenly over baked crust; sprinkle with peanuts. Refrigerate until topping firms slightly (about 15 minutes); then cut into bars about 1 by 2 inches. Store, covered, in refrigerator.

*Makes about 4 1/2 dozen*

# Cookie Brittle

*This delectable confection—an unusual recipe that's part cookie and part candy—is studded with bits of almond brickle.*

1/2 cup (1/4 lb.) butter
  or margarine, softened
3/4 tsp. vanilla
1 cup all-purpose flour
1/2 cup sugar
1 package (6 oz.) almond
  brickle bits

In large bowl of an electric mixer, beat butter and vanilla until creamy. Blend in flour and sugar, then stir in brickle bits (mixture will be quite crumbly).

Spread mixture evenly over bottom of an ungreased 9- by 13-inch baking pan. Lay a piece of wax paper on top and press firmly to pack crumbs evenly. Discard paper.

Bake in a 375° oven for 15 to 20 minutes or until golden around edges. Let brittle cool in pan on a rack for 10 minutes; then loosen with a wide spatula, turn out onto rack, and let cool completely. Break into pieces. Store airtight for up to 2 days; freeze for longer storage.

*Makes about 3 dozen
1 1/2- by 2-inch chunks*

# Banana Squares

Paired with cold milk, these banana-flavored treats
are the perfect thing to satisfy after-school appetites. Each square
is studded with butterscotch chips (or raisins, if you prefer).

6 Tbsp. butter or
  margarine, softened
1 cup firmly packed
  brown sugar
1 egg
1/2 tsp. vanilla
1 large banana, mashed
1 3/4 cups all-purpose flour
1 1/2 tsp. baking powder
1/2 tsp. salt
1/2 cup chopped walnuts
1 package (6 oz.) butter-
  scotch-flavored chips
  or 1 cup raisins

In large bowl of an electric mixer, beat butter and
sugar until creamy; beat in egg, vanilla, and banana.
In another bowl, stir together flour, baking powder,
and salt; gradually add to butter mixture, blending
thoroughly. Stir in walnuts and butterscotch chips.

Spread batter evenly in a greased 9-inch square
baking pan. Bake in a 350° oven for 35 to 40 minutes or until golden brown. Let cool in pan on a rack,
then cut into 2 1/4-inch squares. Store airtight.

*Makes 16*

# Dream Bars

*O*ur version of dream bars includes a sweet orange frosting;
some cookie connoisseurs wouldn't dream of skipping it, while the purists
among us generally prefer their dream bars plain.

⅓ cup butter or
  softened
1½ cups firmly packed
  brown sugar
1 cup plus 2 Tbsp.
  all-purpose flour
2 eggs
1 tsp. vanilla
½ tsp. salt
1 tsp. baking powder
1½ cups shredded coconut
1 cup chopped nuts
Orange Butter Frosting
  (recipe on page 5)

Using an electric mixer, beat butter and ½ cup sugar
until creamy. With a fork, blend in 1 cup flour until
mixture resembles fine crumbs; press firmly over bottom of a greased 9- by 13-inch baking pan. Bake in
a 375° oven for 10 minutes; let cool in pan on a rack.

Clean mixer bowl. Beat eggs until light and lemon-
colored; then gradually beat in remaining 1 cup sugar.
Beat in vanilla, remaining 2 tablespoons flour, salt,
and baking powder. Stir in coconut and nuts.

Pour coconut mixture over crust; spread evenly.
Return to oven; bake for 20 minutes or until topping
is golden. Let cool in pan on a rack for 10 to 15
minutes. Cut partially cooled cookies into bars
(about 1½ by 2 or 1½ by 3 inches), but do not
remove from pan. Spread Orange Butter Frosting
over cookies and let cool completely in pan on rack.
(Don't frost cookies *before* cutting them or frosting
will crack.) Store covered.

*Makes 2 to 3 dozen*

# HAND-MOLDED COOKIES

## Favorite Peanut Butter Cookies

Among the best-known—and best-loved—of cookies are
these traditional treats with their distinctive
crisscrossed tops.

1 cup (1/2 lb.) butter
  or margarine, softened
1 cup peanut butter
1 cup firmly packed
  brown sugar
1 cup granulated sugar
2 eggs
1 tsp. vanilla
3 1/2 cups all-purpose flour
1 tsp. baking soda

In large bowl of an electric mixer, beat butter until
creamy. Gradually beat in peanut butter, then brown
sugar, then granulated sugar. Beat in eggs, then vanilla.

In another bowl, stir together flour and baking
soda; gradually add to the butter mixture, blending
thoroughly. Roll dough into 1-inch balls and place
2 inches apart on greased baking sheets. Press balls
down with a fork, making a crisscross pattern on top
of each with fork tines.

Bake in a 375° oven for 10 to 12 minutes or until
golden brown. Let cool on baking sheets for about a
minute, then transfer to racks. Let cool completely.
Store airtight.

*Makes about 7 dozen*

# Italian Fruit Cookies

*An Italian inclination is to dunk a cookie into wine*
*or coffee before eating, so it comes as no surprise that*
*twice-baked Italian cookies are crunchy.*

2 cups sugar
1 cup (¹/₂ lb.) butter
  or margarine, melted
¹/₄ cup anise seeds
¹/₄ cup anisette or other
  anise-flavored liqueur
3 Tbsp. whiskey, or 2 tsp.
  vanilla and 2 Tbsp. water
6 eggs
5¹/₂ cups all-purpose flour
3 tsp. baking powder
1¹/₂ cups diced mixed
  candied fruit
¹/₂ cup pine nuts or
  slivered almonds

In a large bowl, stir together sugar, butter, anise seeds, anisette, and whiskey. Beat in eggs. In another bowl, stir together flour and baking powder; gradually add to sugar mixture, blending thoroughly. Mix in candied fruit and nuts. Cover tightly with plastic wrap and refrigerate for 2 to 3 hours.

Directly on greased baking sheets, shape dough with your hands to form flat loaves about ¹/₂ inch thick, 2 inches wide, and as long as baking sheets. Place loaves parallel and 4 inches apart. Bake in a 375° oven for 20 minutes or until lightly browned.

Remove loaves from oven and let cool on baking sheets until you can touch them; then cut diagonally into ¹/₂ to ³/₄-inch-thick slices. Place slices close together, cut sides down, on baking sheets. Bake in a 375° oven for 12 to 15 more minutes or until lightly toasted. Transfer to racks to cool. Store airtight.

*Makes about 9 dozen*

# Peanut Blossom Cookies

*Each of these thick, chewy peanut butter cookies has a decorative and tasty chocolate candy kiss right in the middle.*

◌

*¹/₂ cup **each** solid vegetable shortening and peanut butter*
*¹/₂ cup **each** granulated sugar and firmly packed brown sugar*
*1 egg*
*1 tsp. vanilla*
*1¹/₃ cups all-purpose flour*
*1 tsp. baking soda*
*¹/₂ tsp. salt*
*¹/₄ cup granulated sugar*
*2¹/₂ to 3 dozen chocolate candy kisses*

In large bowl of an electric mixer, beat shortening, peanut butter, the ¹/₂ cup granulated sugar, and the brown sugar until creamy; beat in egg and vanilla. In another bowl, stir together flour, baking soda, and salt; gradually add to shortening mixture, blending thoroughly.

Place the ¹/₄ cup granulated sugar in a small bowl. Roll dough into 1-inch balls, then roll in sugar to coat. Place balls 2 inches apart on greased baking sheets.

Bake in a 350° oven for 10 minutes; meanwhile, unwrap chocolate kisses. Remove cookies from oven and quickly top each with a kiss, pressing down until cookie cracks around edges. Return to oven and bake for 3 to 5 more minutes or until cookies are lightly browned and firm to the touch. Transfer to racks and let cool completely. Store airtight.

*Makes 2¹/₂ to 3 dozen*

# Pirouettes

*Rolled into graceful scrolls while still warm, these delicate, lemon-scented cookies make an elegant accompaniment to chocolate mousse or fruit sorbet.*

6 Tbsp. butter or
  margarine, softened
1 cup powdered sugar
2/3 cup all-purpose flour
1/2 tsp. grated lemon zest
1 tsp. vanilla
4 egg whites

In small bowl of an electric mixer, beat butter and sugar until creamy. Gradually add flour and lemon zest and beat until well combined; then add vanilla and egg whites and beat until batter is smooth.

Bake cookies four at a time. First, drop four 1 1/2-teaspoon portions well apart on a well-greased baking sheet; then spread each thinly with a spatula or knife to make an oblong about 3 by 4 inches. Bake in a 425° oven for 3 minutes or until edges begin to brown.

Remove from oven and quickly roll each cookie lengthwise around a wooden spoon handle or chopstick to form a scroll. (If your fingers are sensitive to heat, wear trim-fitting cotton gloves to protect them.) Slide cookie off spoon handle and let cool on a rack. Repeat baking and rolling until all batter is used. Store airtight.

*Makes about 3 dozen*

# Norwegian Kringle

*Hard-cooked egg yolks lend
extra richness to the dough for "kringle," Norway's
pretzel-shaped butter cookies.*

1 cup (¹/₂ lb.) butter,
    softened
1 cup sugar
1 egg
2 hard-cooked egg yolks,
    finely mashed
1 tsp. vanilla
3 cups all-purpose flour
¹/₄ tsp. salt
1 egg white, lightly beaten
Granulated sugar or coarse-
    ly crushed sugar cubes

In large bowl of an electric mixer, beat butter and the
1 cup sugar until creamy; beat in egg, egg yolks, and
vanilla until mixture is well combined. In another
bowl, stir together flour and salt; gradually add to
butter mixture, blending thoroughly. Wrap dough in
plastic wrap and refrigerate for at least 1 hour or
until next day.

Pinch off 1-inch balls of dough and roll each into
a 6-inch-long strand. Form each strand into a pretzel
shape on greased baking sheets, spacing pretzels
about an inch apart. Using a pastry brush, brush
cookies with egg white; then sprinkle with sugar.

Bake in a 350° oven for 12 to 15 minutes or until
pale golden brown. Transfer to racks and let cool
completely. Store airtight.

*Makes about 4 dozen*

# Finnish Ribbon Cakes

*For holiday (or everyday) entertaining, offer a platter of assorted Scandinavian cookies: Swedish Ginger Thins (page 43), Norwegian Kringle (page 27), and these fancy Finnish morsels.*

∽

1 cup (½ lb.) butter
  or margarine, softened
½ cup sugar
1 egg yolk
1 tsp. vanilla
½ tsp. grated lemon zest
2½ cups all-purpose flour
¼ tsp. salt
About 6 Tbsp. raspberry
  or apricot jam
½ cup powdered sugar
  mixed with 1 Tbsp. water

In large bowl of an electric mixer, beat butter and sugar until creamy; beat in egg yolk, vanilla, and lemon zest. In another bowl, stir together flour and salt. Add to butter mixture, blending thoroughly.

Shape dough into ropes ¾ inch in diameter and as long as your baking sheets; place about 2 inches apart on ungreased baking sheets. With the side of your little finger, press a long groove down the center of each rope (but not all the way down to baking sheets). Bake cookies in a 375° oven for 10 minutes.

Remove cookies from oven and spoon jam into the groves. Return to oven for 5 to 10 minutes or until cookies are firm to touch and light golden brown. While cookies are hot, drizzle them with powdered sugar mixture (or spread mixture along sides of cookies). Then cut at a 45° angle into 1-inch lengths. Let cool briefly on baking sheets; transfer to racks and let cool completely. Store airtight.

*Makes about 4 dozen*

*C O O K I E S*

# Chocolate Chews

*Satisfying a chocolate lover is never easy,
but these dark, sugary cookies can help. Their crinkly
tops and chewy texture will delight one and all.*

1 package (6 oz.)
  *semisweet chocolate chips*
*¹/₂ cup (¹/₄ lb.) butter*
  *or margarine, softened*
*1¹/₄ cups sugar*
*2 eggs*
*2 cups all-purpose flour*
*¹/₄ tsp. salt*
*¹/₂ tsp. **each** baking powder*
  *and baking soda*

In top of a double boiler over simmering water, or in
a small pan over lowest possible heat, stir chocolate
chips just until melted; set aside. In large bowl of an
electric mixer, beat butter and 1 cup of the sugar
until creamy; beat in eggs and melted chocolate. In
another bowl, stir together flour, salt, baking powder,
and baking soda; gradually add to butter mixture,
blending thoroughly.

Place remaining ¹/₄ cup sugar in a small bowl.
Roll dough into 1-inch balls and roll in sugar to coat;
place at least 2 inches apart on greased baking sheets.
Bake in a 350° oven for 12 to 14 minutes or until
tops appear dry. Let cool on baking sheets for about
a minute, then transfer to racks and let cool completely. Store airtight.

*Makes about 3¹/₂ dozen*

# Almond Crescents

*A snowy mantle of powdered sugar cloaks these buttery, brandy-spiked nut cookies. Called "kourabiedes," they're a Greek specialty—but they have close cousins in other cuisines, such as Mexican wedding cakes and Russian teacakes.*

⊂⊃

*1/2 cup ground almonds*
*1 cup (1/2 lb.) unsalted butter or margarine, softened*
*1 egg yolk*
*2 Tbsp. powdered sugar*
*1 Tbsp. brandy or 1/2 tsp. vanilla*
*2 cups all-purpose flour*
*1/2 tsp. baking powder*
*11/2 to 2 cups powdered sugar*

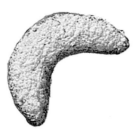

Spread almonds in a shallow pan and toast in a 350° oven for 6 to 8 minutes or until lightly browned. Let cool completely.

In large bowl of an electric mixer, beat butter until creamy. Add egg yolk and the 2 tablespoons powdered sugar; mix well. Stir in brandy and almonds. In another bowl, stir together flour and baking powder. Add to butter mixture gradually, blending thoroughly.

Pinch off dough in 1-inch balls and roll each into a 3-inch rope. Place ropes about 2 inches apart on ungreased baking sheets; shape into crescents. Bake in a 325° oven for 30 minutes or until very lightly browned. Place baking sheets on racks and let cookies cool for 5 minutes.

Sift half the remaining powdered sugar over a sheet of wax paper. Transfer cookies to paper, placing them in a single layer. Sift remaining powdered sugar over cookies to cover. Let cool; store airtight.

*Makes about 21/2 dozen*

# Chocolate-dipped Hazelnut Bonbons

*Add variety to a cookie tray with these chewy, no-bake bonbons made from toasted hazelnuts. If you prefer, you can use whole blanched almonds in place of hazelnuts; you'll need 3 cups.*

1 lb. (3½ cups)
   hazelnuts (filberts),
   whole or in large pieces
2 cups powdered sugar
5 to 6 Tbsp. egg whites
   (whites of about
   3 large eggs)
About 6 oz. semisweet
   chocolate chips

Bake hazelnuts in a 350° oven for 10 to 15 minutes, shaking pan occasionally. Rub briskly with a dishcloth to remove skins. Let cool, then coarsely chop. In a food processor or blender, finely grind nuts, about ⅓ at a time, until mealy. Combine all nuts, sugar and 5 tablespoons egg whites, and process until a paste forms; add more egg whites if needed. (Or mix with a heavy-duty mixer on low speed.) If mixture is too soft to shape, refrigerate in plastic wrap for about 1 hour.

Roll into 1-inch balls; set on wax paper, pressing balls down to flatten bottoms slightly.

In top of a double boiler over simmering water, stir chocolate chips just until melted. Dip each ball (by hand) into chocolate to cover top half; return to wax paper, chocolate side up. Refrigerate, uncovered, until chocolate is set (about 30 minutes). Serve at once, or cover and refrigerate for up to 1 week; let stand at room temperature for 15 minutes before serving.

*Makes 3 to 4 dozen*

# Thumbprint Cookies

*C O O K I E S*

*A* sweet "jewel" of jelly sparkles in the center of each of these nutty morsels. It rests in a small indentation made by your thumb or the tip of a spoon.

⌒

1 cup (½ lb.) butter
  or margarine, softened
½ cup firmly packed
  brown sugar
2 eggs
½ tsp. vanilla
2½ cups all-purpose flour
¼ tsp. salt
1½ cups finely chopped
  walnuts
3 to 4 Tbsp. red currant
  jelly or raspberry jam

In a large bowl, beat butter and sugar until creamy. Separate eggs. Place whites in a small bowl, lightly beat, and set aside; then beat yolks and vanilla into butter mixture. In another bowl, stir together flour and salt. Add to butter mixture; blend thoroughly. With your hands, roll dough into 1-inch balls.

Next, follow steps below. Bake in a 375° oven for 12 to 15 minutes or until lightly browned. Let cool on baking sheets for about a minute, then transfer to racks and let cool completely. Store airtight.

*Makes about 3½ dozen*

**1.** *Dip each ball in egg whites, then roll in walnuts. Place on greased baking sheets.*

**2.** *With your thumb or the tip of a spoon, make an indentation in center of each ball.*

**3.** *Neatly fill each indentation with about ¼ teaspoon red currant jelly or raspberry jam.*

**1.** *Pinch off balls of dough about 1 inch in diameter, then roll each into a 7-inch strand.*

**2.** *Fold strand in half lengthwise. Holding one end in each hand, twist ends in opposite directions.*

**3.** *Brush lightly with egg yolk mixture. This helps sesame seeds stick and gives rich golden color.*

# Koulourakia

$A$t Eastertime in Greece, these sesame-topped cookies
are enjoyed by the dozen. Like shortbread, they're crunchy,
buttery, and not too sweet.

½ cup (¼ lb.) butter
  or margarine, softened
½ cup sugar
3 egg yolks
¼ cup half-and-half
  (light cream)
2¼ cups all-purpose flour
1 tsp. baking powder
¼ tsp. salt
2 to 3 Tbsp. sesame seeds

In large bowl of an electric mixer, beat butter and
sugar until creamy. Beat in 2 of the egg yolks, one at
a time. Mix in 3 tablespoons of the half-and-half.
In another bowl, stir together flour, baking powder,
and salt; gradually add to butter mixture, blending
thoroughly.

To shape cookies, pinch off 1-inch balls of dough;
roll each into a 7-inch strand. Bring ends together
and twist (see photo 2 on facing page) or form into
a pretzel shape. Place slightly apart on greased baking sheets. Beat remaining egg yolk with remaining
1 tablespoon half-and-half; brush lightly over cookies and sprinkle with sesame seeds. Bake in a 350°
oven for about 15 minutes or until golden. Transfer
to racks and let cook completely. Store airtight.

Makes about 2½ dozen

COOKIES

# SPECIALTY COOKIES

## Sugar Cookies

Why do children love sugar cookies so much?
Maybe it's because of their flavor, and maybe it's because they
can be cut into so many shapes.

*3/4 cup (1/4 lb. plus 4 Tbsp.)
   butter or margarine,
   softened*
*1 cup sugar*
*2 eggs*
*1 tsp. vanilla*
*2 3/4 cups all-purpose flour*
*1 tsp. **each** baking powder
   and salt*
*Sugar*

Using an electric mixer, beat butter and 1 cup sugar
until creamy; beat in eggs and vanilla. In another bowl,
combine flour, baking powder, and salt; blend with
butter mixture to form a soft dough. Cover tightly with
plastic wrap and refrigerate until firm (at least 1 hour).

On a floured board, roll out dough, a portion at a
time, to a thickness of 1/8 inch (keep remaining portions refrigerated). Cut out with cookie cutters (about
2 1/2 inches in diameter) and place slightly apart on
ungreased baking sheets. Sprinkle with sugar.

Bake in a 400° oven for 8 to 10 minutes or until
edges are lightly browned. Transfer to racks and let
cool completely before handling. Store airtight.

*Makes about 4 dozen*

# Flaky Fruit Turnovers

$A$ *rich butter pastry distinguishes these tender, triangular turnover cookies; tucked inside is a dried-fruit filling made of apricots. The cookies freeze well, so consider baking a batch to put away.*

2 cups all-purpose flour
1/4 cup sugar
1 cup (1/2 lb.) firm butter
   or margarine, cut
   into pieces
1/3 cup milk
1/2 cup firmly packed
   chopped dried apricots
2/3 cup water
1/4 cup firmly packed
   brown sugar

In a bowl, combine flour and sugar. Add butter; with your fingers or a pastry blender, rub or cut mixture until fine, even crumbs form. Gradually add milk, mixing with a fork until dough holds together. Cover tightly with plastic wrap and refrigerate for 30 minutes to 1 hour. Meanwhile, prepare the filling: In a small pan, combine apricots, water, and brown sugar. Cook over medium heat, stirring constantly and mashing with a spoon, until mixture forms a smooth, thick paste (about 10 minutes). Cool to room temperature.

Divide dough in half; form each half into a ball. On a well-floured board, roll out one ball into a 12-inch square, then cut into sixteen 3-inch squares (press straight down with long-bladed knife to make neat cookies). Mound a scant teaspoon of filling in center of each square. Fold each over into a triangle; seal by running a pastry wheel around edges or crimping them with the tines of a fork. Repeat with remaining dough.

Transfer cookies to ungreased baking sheets. If desired, use a small, sharp knife to cut a small slash in each cookie to expose filling. Bake in a 350° oven for 18 to 20 minutes or until golden brown. Transfer to racks and let cool. Store airtight.

*Makes 32*

*C O O K I E S*

# Finnish Rye Cookies

*Rye flour gives these cookies an unusual nutty flavor. The shape is
a bit unusual, too—each thin round has a small, off-center hole cut in it.
In Finland, they're a Christmas tradition known as "ruiskakut".*

1 cup rye flour
1/2 cup all-purpose flour
1/4 tsp. salt
1/2 cup sugar
1/2 cup (1/4 lb.) firm butter
  or margarine, cut into
  pieces
4 Tbsp. milk

In a bowl, stir together rye flour, all-purpose flour, salt, and sugar. Add butter and rub with your fingers until mixture forms fine, even crumbs. Add milk, 1 tablespoon at a time, stirring with a fork until stiff dough forms. Gather dough into a ball, wrap tightly in plastic wrap, and refrigerate for 1 hour.

On a floured board, roll out dough, a portion at a time, to a thickness of about 1/8 inch. Cut out with a round cookie cutter (about 2 1/2 inches in diameter). Then cut a hole slightly off center in each cookie, using a tiny round cutter about 1/2 inch in diameter. (You can use the cap from a vanilla or other extract bottle.) Place slightly apart on lightly greased baking sheets; prick each cookie several times with a fork.

Bake in a 375° oven for 8 to 10 minutes or until cookies are lightly browned and firm to the touch. (You can bake the little cut-out holes, too—or reroll them to make more cookies.) Transfer baked cookies to racks and let cool. Store airtight.

*Makes about 2 1/2 dozen*

# Viennese Jam Rounds

*These fancy cookies resemble stained-glass windows; before baking, each one is crowned with a bit of jam and two crisscrossed dough strips.*

∽

1 cup (1/2 lb.) butter
  or margarine, softened
1 cup sugar
2 egg yolks
1 tsp. grated lemon zest
2 cups all-purpose flour
1/4 tsp. salt
3/4 tsp. ground cinnamon
1/4 tsp. ground cloves
1 cup ground almonds
About 1/2 cup raspberry
  or apricot jam

In large bowl of an electric mixer, beat butter and sugar until creamy. Beat in egg yolks and lemon zest. In another bowl, stir together flour, salt, cinnamon, and cloves; gradually add to butter mixture, blending thoroughly. Stir in almonds (dough will be very stiff). Gather dough into a ball, wrap tightly in plastic wrap, and refrigerate for 1 hour.

Divide dough in half. Roll each half between 2 pieces of wax paper to a thickness of 1/8 inch. Cut out with a 2-inch round cookie cutter and place about 2 inches apart on ungreased baking sheets. Top each cookie with about 1/2 teaspoon jam, spreading to within about 1/2 inch of edges. Cut dough scraps (reroll, if necessary) into 1/4 by 2-inch strips; cross 2 strips over top of each cookie and press ends down lightly.

Bake in a 375° oven for about 12 minutes or until edges are browned. Let cool for about a minute on baking sheets, then transfer to racks and let cool completely. Store airtight.

*Makes about 4 dozen*

*C O O K I E S*

# Almond Ravioli Cookies

We borrowed a tradi-
tional technique from
Italian cooking to
make these tasty little
almond-filled bites.

1 cup (½ lb.) butter or
  margarine, softened
1½ cups powdered sugar
1 egg
1 tsp. vanilla
2½ cups all-purpose flour
1 tsp. **each** baking soda
  and cream of tartar
About ⅔ cup (6 oz.)
  almond paste
About ⅓ cup sliced almonds

Using an electric mixer, beat butter and sugar until
creamy; beat in egg and vanilla. In another bowl,
stir together flour, baking soda, and cream of tartar;
gradually add to butter mixture. Divide dough in
half. Wrap each half tightly in plastic wrap; refrigerate until firm (2 to 3 hours) or for up to 3 days.

Place one dough portion between 2 pieces of wax
paper and roll out into a 10- by 15-inch rectangle.
Peel off and discard top paper. With a pastry wheel
or a long-bladed knife, lightly mark dough into 1-inch
squares. Place a scant ¼ teaspoon of almond paste in
center of each square; refrigerate while rolling top layer.

Roll out second portion of dough. Discard top
paper. Invert sheet of dough onto almond-paste-
topped dough. Discard second paper. Gently press
top layer of dough around mounds of filling.

Flour pastry wheel or knife and cut filled dough
into 1-inch squares; run pastry wheel around outer
edges to seal (or press with fingers). Place cookies
1 inch apart on ungreased baking sheets. Push a sliced
almond diagonally into the center of each cookie.

Bake in a 350° oven for 10 to 12 minutes or until
golden. Transfer to racks and let cool. Store airtight.

*Makes about 12½ dozen*

# Fructose Spice Cookies

Baked goods made with fructose are moister
and brown more readily than those made with sucrose.
Try this specifically designed recipe for soft, chewy spice cookies.

1 cup granulated fructose
1/2 cup (1/4 lb.) butter or
   margarine, melted
2 eggs, lightly beaten
1 tsp. grated lemon zest
2 tsp. vanilla
1 cup **each** all-purpose flour
   and whole wheat flour
1 tsp. cream of tartar
1/2 tsp. baking soda
1 1/2 tsp. ground cinnamon
1/4 tsp. **each** ground
   nutmeg and salt
1/8 tsp. ground cloves

In a large bowl, stir together fructose and butter; mix in eggs, lemon zest, and vanilla. In another bowl, stir together all-purpose flour, whole wheat flour, cream of tartar, baking soda, cinnamon, nutmeg, salt and cloves; add to egg mixture and stir until blended. Cover dough tightly with plastic wrap and refrigerate until firm (about 2 hours).

Force dough through a cookie press to form round shapes, spacing cookies about 1½ inches apart on greased baking sheets. (Or drop rounded teaspoonfuls of dough 1½ inches apart.) Bake in a 350° oven for 10 to 12 minutes or until firm to the touch. transfer to racks and let cool. Store airtight.

*Makes 4 to 5 dozen*

# Swedish Ginger Thins

*Very spicy, very dark, very thin, and very crisp—these cookies can be cut into fancy shapes.*

2/3 cup butter or margarine

1/3 cup **each** granulated sugar and firmly packed brown sugar

2 Tbsp. dark corn syrup

2 tsp. **each** ground ginger and cloves

3 tsp. ground cinnamon

2 tsp. baking soda

1/4 cup water

2 1/2 cups all-purpose flour

Royal Icing (recipe on page 5) or decorating icing in a tube

In a medium-size pan, combine butter, granulated sugar, brown sugar, and corn syrup; place over medium heat and stir until butter is melted. Remove from heat, stir in ginger, cloves, and cinnamon, and let cool slightly. Stir baking soda into water and add to butter mixture, blending thoroughly. Then stir in flour until well combined (dough will be quite soft). Cover tightly with plastic wrap and refrigerate until firm (2 to 3 hours) or for up to 3 days.

On a floured board, roll out dough, a portion at a time, to a thickness of about 1/16 inch. Cut out with cookie cutters (about 2 1/2 inches in diameter). If necessary, dip cutters in flour to prevent dough from sticking to them. Place cookies slightly apart on ungreased baking sheets. Bake in a 325° oven for 10 to 12 minutes or until slightly darker brown and firm to the touch. Transfer to racks and let cool completely.

If desired, press Royal Icing through a decorating tube with a plain tip, making swirls and outline designs on cookies. Let icing dry before storing cookies. Store airtight.

*Makes about 5 dozen*

COOKIES

# ICEBOX COOKIES

## Danish Sugar Cookies

*Denmark is well known for the quality of her pastry and cookies, and these special little treats will show you why.*

1 cup sugar
½ cup (¼ lb.) firm butter, cut into pieces
½ cup whole blanched almonds, finely ground
1 tsp. vanilla
1 cup all-purpose flour
Sugar

Place the 1 cup sugar in a large bowl; cut in butter with a pastry blender or 2 knives until mixture forms fine particles. Stir in almonds and vanilla. Blend in flour, mixing with your hands if necessary, until well combined. Shape dough into a roll 1½ inches in diameter. Sprinkle a little sugar (1 to 2 tablespoons) on a sheet of wax paper; then place roll of dough on paper and wrap snugly, coating outside of roll with sugar. Refrigerate until firm (at least 2 hours) or for up to 3 days.

Unwrap dough. Using a sharp knife, cut into ⅛-inch-thick slices. Place slices slightly apart on ungreased baking sheets. Bake in a 375° oven for 8 to 10 minutes or until lightly browned. Let cool on baking sheets for about a minute, then transfer to racks and let cool completely. Store airtight.

*Makes about 5 dozen*

# Spiced Almond Thins

*Sour cream, brown sugar, cinnamon, and nutmeg combine in a crisp spice wafer with an appealing old-fashioned flavor. Crunchy bits of almond give the cookies a pebbly appearance.*

1 cup (½ lb.) butter
  or margarine, softened
1 cup firmly packed
  brown sugar
2 cups all-purpose flour
2 tsp. ground cinnamon
½ tsp. ground nutmeg
¼ tsp. baking soda
¼ cup sour cream
½ cup slivered blanched
  almonds

In large bowl of an electric mixer, beat butter and sugar until creamy. In another bowl, stir together flour, cinnamon, and nutmeg. Stir baking soda into sour cream; add to butter mixture alternately with flour mixture, blending thoroughly. Stir in almonds until well combined. Shape dough into a 2½-inch-thick rectangular log; wrap in wax paper and refrigerate until firm (at least 2 hours) or for up to 3 days.

Unwrap dough. Using a sharp knife, cut into ⅛-inch-thick slices; place slices about 1 inch apart on ungreased baking sheets. Bake in a 350° oven for 10 minutes or until golden brown. Let cool for about a minute on baking sheets, then transfer to racks and let cool completely. Store airtight.

*Makes about 5 dozen*

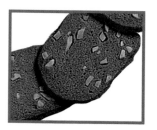

# Lemon-Pecan Wafers

*Here's a good summertime cookie.*
*Though rich with butter and nuts, it has a refreshing,*
*lemony sparkle.*

꩜

1/2 cup (1/4 lb.) butter
 or margarine, softened
1 cup sugar
1 egg
1 Tbsp. **each** grated lemon
 zest and lemon juice
2 cups all-purpose flour
1/8 tsp. salt
1 tsp. baking powder
1 cup chopped pecans.

In large bowl of an electric mixer, beat butter and
sugar until creamy; beat in egg, lemon zest, and
lemon juice. In another bowl, stir together flour, salt,
and baking powder; gradually add to butter mixture,
blending thoroughly. Stir in pecans, mixing with
your hands if necessary to distribute nuts evenly.
Shape dough into 2 rolls, each 1 1/2 inches in diameter; wrap in wax paper and refrigerate until firm
(at least 2 hours) or for up to 3 days.

Unwrap dough. Using a sharp knife, cut into
1/8-inch-thick slices; place slices about 1 inch apart
on greased baking sheets. Bake in a 350° oven
for 12 minutes or until edges are lightly browned.
Transfer to racks and let cool. Store airtight.

*Makes about 6 dozen*

# Peanut Pinwheels

In this recipe, a ribbon of chocolate winds its way through the center of a crisp peanut butter cookie.

½ cup (¼ lb.) butter
   or margarine, softened
½ cup creamy peanut butter
½ cup **each** granulated
   sugar and firmly packed
   brown sugar
1 egg
1¼ cups all-purpose flour
½ tsp. **each** baking soda,
   salt, and ground cinnamon
1 package (6 oz.) semisweet
   chocolate chips

In large bowl of an electric mixer, beat butter, peanut butter, granulated sugar, and brown sugar until creamy; beat in egg. In another bowl, stir together flour, baking soda, salt, and cinnamon; gradually add to butter mixture; blend thoroughly. Cover tightly with plastic wrap and refrigerate until firm (about 2 hours).

In top of a double boiler over simmering water or in a small pan over lowest possible heat, melt chocolate chips, stirring constantly. Let cool slightly. On wax paper, pat chilled dough out into a 12-inch square. Spread chocolate evenly over dough to within ½ inch of edges. Roll up jelly roll style; then cut in half crosswise. Wrap each roll in wax paper and refrigerate until firm (at least 2 hours) or for up to 3 days.

Remove one roll from refrigerator. Unwrap; using a sharp knife, cut into ¼-inch-thick slices. Place slices about 1 inch apart on ungreased baking sheets. Bake in a 375° oven for about 10 minutes or until lightly browned. Let cool on baking sheets for 2 or 3 minutes, then transfer to racks and let cool completely. Repeat with second roll of dough. Store airtight.

*Makes about 4 dozen*

C O O K I E S

# Coconut Shortbread Cookies

Is it possible to improve on traditional Scottish shortbread? One taste of these meltingly rich cookies may convince you to answer "yes." Lots of coconut is added to a basic shortbread dough for an irresistible cross-cultural treat.

1 cup (½ lb.) butter,
  softened
¼ cup granulated sugar
1 tsp. vanilla
2 cups all-purpose flour
¼ tsp. salt
2 cups flaked coconut
About 1 cup powdered sugar

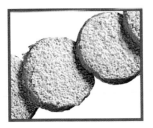

In large bowl of an electric mixer, beat butter until creamy; add granulated sugar and beat until smooth. Mix in vanilla. In another bowl, stir together flour and salt; gradually add to butter mixture, blending thoroughly. Add coconut and mix until well combined. Shape dough into a roll about 1½ inches in diameter; wrap in wax paper and refrigerate until firm (at least 2 hours) or for up to 3 days.

Unwrap dough. Using a sharp knife, cut into ¼-inch-thick slices; place slices slightly apart on ungreased baking sheets. Bake in a 300° oven for 20 minutes or until cookies are firm to the touch and lightly browned on bottoms. Transfer to racks and let cool for 5 minutes. Sift half the powdered sugar onto wax paper and transfer cookies to it in a single layer; sift additional powdered sugar on top to cover cookies lightly. Let cookies cool completely. Store airtight.

*Makes about 4 dozen*

# Poppy Seed Nut Slices

*Hazelnuts and poppy seeds team up to give these crunchy little cookies their distinctive flavor. If you like hazelnuts, you might also enjoy the chocolate-dipped bonbons on page 31.*

1 cup (½ lb.) butter or
  margarine, softened
1 cup sugar
1 egg
1 tsp. vanilla
2½ cups all-purpose flour
⅓ cup poppy seeds
½ tsp. ground cinnamon
¼ tsp. **each** salt and ground
  ginger
1½ cups coarsely chopped
  hazelnuts (filberts)

In large bowl of an electric mixer, beat butter and sugar until creamy; beat in egg and vanilla. In another bowl, stir together flour, poppy seeds, cinnamon, salt, and ginger; gradually add to butter mixture, blending thoroughly. Add hazelnuts, mixing with your hands if necessary to distribute nuts evenly. Shape dough into 2 or 3 rolls, each 1½ inches in diameter; wrap in wax paper and refrigerate until firm (at least 2 hours) or for up to 3 days.

Unwrap dough. Using a sharp knife, cut into ¼-inch-thick slices; place slices about 1 inch apart on ungreased baking sheets. Bake in a 350° oven for 12 to 15 minutes or until edges are golden. Transfer to racks and let cool. Store airtight.

*Makes about 7 dozen*

# Date-Oatmeal Cookies

*When you bite into these cookies,
you'll find a delectable combination of flavors:
oats, nuts, dates, and a subtle touch of cinnamon.*

1 cup (½ lb.) butter
  or margarine, softened
1 cup sugar
1 tsp. vanilla
2 eggs
1¾ cups all-purpose flour
1 tsp. **each** baking powder
  and ground cinnamon
¾ tsp. baking soda
½ tsp. salt
2 cups quick-cooking
  rolled oats
8 oz. whole pitted dates
  (1½ cups lightly packed)
1 cup chopped pecans
  or walnuts

In large bowl of an electric mixer, beat butter and sugar until creamy. Beat in vanilla; then beat in eggs, one at a time. In another bowl, stir together flour, baking powder, cinnamon, baking soda, and salt; gradually add to butter mixture, blending thoroughly. Stir in oats, dates, and pecans, mixing well and distributing dates evenly through dough. Shape dough into 2 or 3 rolls, each 1¾ inches in diameter; wrap in wax paper and refrigerate until firm (at least 4 hours) or for up to 3 days.

Unwrap dough. Using a sharp knife, cut into ¼-inch-thick slices; place slices about 1 inch apart on ungreased baking sheets. Bake in a 375° oven for 10 to 12 minutes or until edges are golden. Transfer to racks and let cool. Store airtight.

*Makes about 6½ dozen*

**1.** Unwrap chilled logs and slice lengthwise into quarters, using a sharp knife.

**2.** Reassemble logs, alternating dark and light portions to make stripes. Press layers together gently as you work.

**3.** With a sharp knife, cut logs crosswise into ⅛-inch-thick slices. If layers start to separate, refrigerate until firmer.

# Black & White Slices

*Jaunty stripes of vanilla and chocolate-flavored dough give these cookies a festive appearance. You can experiment by combining the doughs into pinwheels or other shapes.*

½ cup (¼ lb.) butter
  or margarine, softened
½ cup sugar
1 egg yolk
1½ cups all-purpose flour
1½ tsp. baking powder
⅛ tsp. salt
3 Tbsp. milk
½ tsp. vanilla
1 square (1 oz.) unsweet-
  ened chocolate

Using an electric mixer, beat butter and sugar until creamy; beat in egg yolk. In another bowl, stir together flour, baking powder, and salt. In a small cup, combine milk and vanilla. Add dry ingredients to butter mixture alternately with milk mixture, blending thoroughly after each addition.

In top of a double boiler over simmering water or in a small pan over lowest possible heat, melt chocolate, stirring constantly; let cool slightly. Divide dough in half; take 1 tablespoon dough from one half and add it to the other half. Stir chocolate into smaller portion of dough, blending well.

Shape each portion of dough into roll 1½ inches in diameter. Wrap each in wax paper; flatten sides, making square logs. Refrigerate until firm (at least 2 hours). Unwrap dough, cut into quarters, and reassemble as shown opposite (Steps 1 and 2).

Slice logs crosswise (Step 3). Place slices about 1 inch apart on greased baking sheets. Bake in a 350° oven for about 10 minutes or until golden. Transfer to racks and let cool. Store airtight.

*Makes about 4 dozen*

COOKIES

# WHOLESOME COOKIES

## *Half-cup Cookies*

*These chunky, down-to-earth drop cookies take their name from the nine (count 'em!) ingredients included in one-half-cup quantity.*

½ cup (¼ lb.) butter
 or margarine, softened
½ cup **each** peanut butter and
 firmly packed brown sugar
2 eggs
½ cup honey
¼ cup milk
½ tsp. vanilla
2 cups whole wheat flour
1 tsp. **each** baking powder
 and ground cinnamon
¾ tsp. salt
½ cup **each** semisweet chocolate chips; toasted almonds
 or walnut pieces; unsweetened flaked coconut; raisins;
 and granola

In large bowl of an electric mixer, beat butter, peanut butter, and sugar until creamy; beat in eggs, honey, milk, and vanilla. In another bowl, stir together flour, baking powder, cinnamon, and salt; gradually add to butter mixture, blending thoroughly. Mix in chocolate chips, nuts, coconut, raisins, and granola until well combined.

Drop dough by rounded tablespoonfuls onto lightly greased baking sheets, spacing cookies about 1 inch apart. Bake in a 375° oven for about 10 minutes or until golden brown. Transfer to racks and let cool. Store airtight.

*Makes about 5 dozen*

# Quick Carob Brownies

When ground and roasted, carob pods yield a brown powder that can be used in baking as a stand-in for unsweetened cocoa. Dress these brownies up with a dusting of powdered sugar.

6 Tbsp. butter or margarine
2 eggs
1 cup granulated sugar
¹/₂ tsp. vanilla
³/₄ cup all-purpose flour
¹/₂ cup roasted carob powder
1 tsp. baking powder
¹/₂ tsp. salt
Powdered sugar

Place butter in an 8-inch square baking pan; set pan in oven while oven preheats to 325°. When butter is melted, remove pan from oven and set aside.

In a large bowl of an electric mixer, beat eggs, granulated sugar, and vanilla until thick and lemon-colored; pour in butter and stir until blended (set baking pan aside unwashed). In another bowl, stir together flour, carob powder, baking powder, and salt; sift into egg mixture and stir just until smoothly blended.

Spread batter in baking pan and bake in a 325° oven for 25 minutes or until a pick inserted in center comes out clean. Place pan on a rack and let cool completely. Sift powdered sugar lightly over top; let cool. Cut into 2-inch squares. Store airtight.

*Makes 16*

# Tahini Cookies

*The sesame-seed paste called tahini is a staple in Middle Eastern cooking, adding rich, nutty flavor to a variety of dishes. Here, we use it in crisp whole wheat cookies topped with toasted sesame seeds.*

½ cup **each** granulated
  sugar and firmly packed
  brown sugar
½ cup tahini
  (stir before measuring)
4 Tbsp. butter or margarine,
  softened
¼ cup solid vegetable
  shortening
1 egg
1⅓ cups whole wheat flour
¾ tsp. baking soda
½ tsp. baking powder
About 3 Tbsp. sesame seeds

In large bowl of an electric mixer, beat granulated sugar, brown sugar, tahini, butter, and shortening until creamy. Beat in egg. In another bowl, stir together flour, baking soda, and baking powder; gradually add to tahini mixture, blending thoroughly. Cover tightly with plastic wrap and refrigerate until easy to handle (about 2 hours) or until next day.

Meanwhile, in a small frying pan over medium heat, toast sesame seeds, shaking pan frequently, until golden (about 2 minutes). Let cool.

Roll dough into 1-inch balls. Dip balls into toasted sesame seeds and press down so seeds adhere to dough; then place balls, seeded side up, about 3 inches apart on ungreased baking sheets. Flatten each ball with a fork dipped in flour, making a criss-cross pattern with fork tines. Bake in a 375° oven for 8 to 10 minutes or until lightly browned. Let cool on baking sheets for 2 minutes; then transfer to racks and let cool completely. Store airtight.

*Makes about 5 dozen*

# Fig Bars

*If you like fruit-filled cookies, you'll love these fig bars. They keep well, becoming softer and more flavorful after a day or so.*

∽

½ cup (¼ lb.) butter or margarine, softened
½ cup **each** granulated sugar and firmly packed brown sugar
2 eggs
½ tsp. vanilla
1 cup whole wheat flour
1¼ cups all-purpose flour
¼ cup toasted unsweetened wheat germ
¼ tsp. **each** salt and baking soda
Fig filling (recipe on page 5)

Using an electric mixer, beat butter, granulated sugar, and brown sugar until creamy. Beat in eggs and vanilla. In another bowl, stir together whole wheat flour, all-purpose flour, wheat germ, salt, and baking soda; gradually add to butter mixture, blend thoroughly. Cover with plastic wrap; refrigerate at least 1 hour.

Divide dough into 2 equal portions. (Return one to refrigerator.) On a floured board, roll out first portion to a 9 by 15-inch rectangle; cut lengthwise into three strips. Divide Fig Filling into 6 equal portions and evenly distribute one portion down center of each strip, bringing it out to ends. Use a long spatula to lift sides of each dough strip over filling, overlapping edges slightly on top. Press together lightly. Cut strips in half crosswise, lift and invert onto greased baking sheets (seam side down). Brush off excess flour. Refrigerate for 15 minutes. Repeat procedure with remaining dough.

Bake in a 375° oven for 15 to 20 minutes or until browned. Cool on baking sheets on a rack for about 10 minutes; then cut each strip crosswise into 4 pieces. Transfer cookies to racks and let cool completely. Store covered.

*Makes 4 dozen*

C O O K I E S

# Date Tarts

*Here, sun-ripened fruits lend their rich flavor and wholesomeness to a fancy filled cookie. We've called it a "date tart" because it resembles a little pie.*

෴

1/2 cup (1/4 lb.) butter or margarine, softened
1 cup firmly packed brown sugar
2 eggs
1 tsp. vanilla
2 cups all-purpose flour
1/2 cup toasted unsweetened wheat germ
1/2 tsp. *each* salt and ground nutmeg
1/4 tsp. baking soda
Date Filling (recipe on page 5)

In large bowl of an electric mixer, beat butter and sugar until creamy; beat in eggs and vanilla. In another bowl, stir together flour, wheat germ, salt, nutmeg, and baking soda; gradually add to butter mixture, blending thoroughly. Cover dough tightly with plastic wrap and refrigerate until easy to handle (at least 2 hours) or for up to 3 days.

Take out a third of the dough, leaving remaining dough in refrigerator. On a well-floured board, roll out dough to a thickness of 1/16 inch; cut out with a 3-inch round cookie cutter. Repeat with remaining dough, rolling and cutting one portion at a time.

Place half the cookies slightly apart on greased baking sheets. Spoon a heaping teaspoonful of Date Filling onto each, cover with another cookie, and press edges together with a floured fork. Slash top. Bake in a 350° oven for 12 to 15 minutes or until lightly browned. Transfer to racks; let cool. Store airtight.

*Makes about 2 1/2 dozen*

# Branapple Bars

*These no-bake cookies are made with bran cereal for an extra-high fiber content. Moist, chewy, and packed with good things—apples, peanut butter, and nuts—you can serve with milk or fruit juice for a nutritious snack or breakfast treat.*

1 package (6 oz.) dried
   apple rings or slices
3 cups boiling water
½ cup sesame seeds
4 cups whole bran cereal
¼ cup toasted unsweetened
   wheat germ
½ cup roasted unsalted sunflower seeds
½ cup chopped walnuts
   or almonds
1 cup honey
1½ cups peanut butter
2 Tbsp. butter or margarine
1 tsp. ground cinnamon

Place dried apples in a medium-size bowl and pour boiling water over them. Let stand for 20 minutes. Meanwhile, in a wide frying pan over medium heat, toast sesame seeds, shaking pan frequently, until golden (about 2 minutes). Let cool; then place in a large mixing bowl and stir in bran cereal, wheat germ, sunflower seeds, and walnuts. Drain apples well; then whirl in a food processor until finely ground (or put through a food chopper fitted with a fine blade). Add to cereal mixture.

In a 2½- to 3-quart pan, cook honey over medium heat until it reaches 230°F on a candy thermometer; stir in peanut butter, butter, and cinnamon. Cook, stirring, until mixture returns to 230°F. Remove from heat and pour over cereal mixture. Stir with a wooden spoon until thoroughly blended.

Turn mixture into a well-greased 10 by 15-inch rimmed baking pan; press down firmly to fill pan evenly. Cover and refrigerate until firm (about 2 hours); then cut into 2 by 2½-inch bars. Wrap individually in foil and store in refrigerator up to 2 weeks.

*Makes 2½ dozen*

# Orange Wheat Cookies

*A crunchy, decorative rim of sesame seeds adds interest to these icebox wafers. Daintier than most whole wheat cookies, they have a pleasing crispness and a delicate orange flavor.*

⌒

1 cup (½ lb.) butter
  or margarine, softened
1 cup firmly packed
  brown sugar
1 egg
1 tsp. grated orange peel
2¼ cups whole wheat flour
1½ cups quick-cooking
  rolled oats
¼ cup sesame seeds

In large bowl of an electric mixer, beat butter and sugar until creamy; beat in egg and orange peel. Gradually add flour and oats, blending thoroughly. Shape dough into 2 rolls, each about 1½ inches in diameter. Evenly sprinkle 2 tablespoons of the sesame seeds on each of 2 sheets of wax paper. Roll each portion of dough in seeds to coat on all sides; then wrap in wax paper and refrigerate until firm (at least 2 hours) or for up to 3 days.

Unwrap dough. Using a sharp knife, cut into ¼-inch-thick slices; place slices about 1 inch apart on ungreased baking sheets. Bake in a 350° oven for 12 to 15 minutes or until lightly browned. Transfer to racks and let cool. Store airtight.

*Makes about 5 dozen*

# Zucchini Bars

*Coarse shreds of zucchini, bits of dried fruit, and coconut make these bar cookies extra moist and chewy. They're topped with chopped walnuts for a crunchy finishing touch.*

⌒

¾ cup (¼ lb. plus 4 Tbsp.) butter or margarine, softened

½ cup **each** granulated sugar and firmly packed brown sugar

2 eggs

2 tsp. vanilla

1¾ cups all-purpose flour

½ tsp. salt

1½ tsp. baking powder

¾ cup **each** unsweetened flaked coconut, snipped pitted dates, and raisins

2 cups unpared, coarsely shredded zucchini

1 Tbsp butter or margarine, melted

2 Tbsp. milk

¼ tsp. ground cinnamon

1 cup powdered sugar

1 cup chopped walnuts

In large bowl of an electric mixer, beat the ¾ cup butter, granulated sugar, and brown sugar until creamy; beat in eggs and 1 teaspoon of the vanilla. In another bowl, stir together flour, salt, and baking powder; gradually add to butter mixture, blending thoroughly. Mix in coconut, dates, raisins, and zucchini until well combined.

Spread batter evenly in a greased 10 by 15-inch rimmed baking pan. Bake in a 350° oven for 35 to 40 minutes or until a pick inserted in center comes out clean. Place on a rack and let cool slightly.

In a small bowl beat together the melted butter, milk, remaining vanilla, cinnamon, and powdered sugar. Drizzle glaze over warm cookies, then spread evenly; sprinkle with walnuts. Let cool completely, then cut into 1½ by 2-inch bars. Store airtight.

*Makes about 4 dozen*